LOVERS
ARE BLIND

DHYAN SOMPURA

"*This one's for you Babiekriii, though you're not here with us, we remember you everyday.*

The one who always supported me and loved my work."

Contents

Contents

"To my baby Rex who never made me feel lonely."

My Baby rex

fierce but soft

loved him as much as i love me

but still couldn't care

to spend time with him

felt meaningless crying later

feeling the guilt of not seeing him earlier

when i was the only one who met him.

karma will surely pass the loneliness to me

and i deserve it but he didn't,

he was innocent, but i'm not

let this happen when i knew

how lonely he was.

May you rest in peace.

Preface

Love, in all its glorious and agonizing facets, is the beating heart of this collection. "Lovers Are Blind" is a journey through the intoxicating highs of connection and the soul-crushing lows of letting go. Within these pages, you'll encounter poems that celebrate the exhilarating rush of first love, explore the vulnerabilities laid bare in intimacy, and offer poignant reflections on the enduring pain of unrequited longing.

This collection is a testament to the complexities of the human heart, reminding us that even in the face of heartbreak, love's enduring power can be both a source of immense joy and profound sorrow. While some of these poems draw inspiration from personal experiences, many are born from the imagination, capturing the universal emotions that arise when we open ourselves to love.

My hope is that these poems will resonate with readers, offering solace and understanding during times of heartbreak. Perhaps they will serve as a reminder that even in the darkest moments, love's enduring power can offer a beacon of hope and the strength to move forward.

Acknowledgements

I would like to acknowledge the readers for supporting me by reading this book, it means the world to me. I would like to thank my Parents, Dushyant Sompura and Janki Sompura for their moral and emotional support and my Grand Parents Suresh Sompura and Jaymanben Sompra for their inspirational support, which raised my confidence for writing and especially my sisters Dhruvi Sompura and Ritvi Sompura for sparing me time to complete this book, just kidding; for actually reviewing my book, supporting my enthusiasm and keeping the environment joyous all the time. They're the ones who light up the family's faces even when there's trouble.

I would like to thank my Friends for reading my book and giving me reviews and comments for the same, especially Diya Sangani, Divyesh Girnari and Niharika solanki who read my primary manuscripts and enjoyed my poetry, which led to completion of this book. I would also like to thank my friend Radhika Limbasiya- the co-author of our first published book "THOSE TINY LITTLE MOMENTS" who guided me from the beginning to write poetry and integrate my thoughts in them; which led a foundation for me to write poetry. I would also like to thank her for sending me photos of Northern lights straight from Canada, and even for helping me with the book cover.

I would like to acknowledge my friend Krishi Jain who is not here with us but would have loved to watch me launch another one. for you babiekrii-

ACKNOWLEDGEMENTS

"you flew away spreading smiles

and departing joy in our lives,

melting our hearts

with flashes of unforgettable memories

you moved ahead with your journey

ascending to the next level

to elevate many new faces with laughter

and changing their lives

with your own krishi vibes

which were as crazy and bravado

as one's life should be.

it's as if an angel came into our lives

appearing as our friend,

teaching us how valuable each moments

are in our lives;

making us regret all those times

we weren't there and thanking

for the moments we were,

turning them into magical memories.

you vanished with your valour

showing us how valuable any relationship is,

whether it's friends or family.

you taught us to explore our freedom

with spreading our wings,

just as you went to explore your own venture;

into the clouds.

and all that's left now are these photos

which turn those happy memories

into golden tears,

just like your brown munde eyes

glittering in the eyes of heaven.

you will always sparkle in our eyes

just like the crackers in diwali

which brightens the nights

dispersing comfort in our hearts

like you did.

it doesn't matter how hard we cry,

how hard we miss or drink

to make us feel better,

you're stuck in our minds

just as souls in our hearts.

it hurts remembering

or even glaring at those pictures

and thinking of those crazy days.

what to do to move on?

there's no way we can't think of you,

and it hurts the most

realising you're not here

and someplace else

where; we don't know.

i know it's selfish to feel this way

but my heart aches not seeing you around,

remembering your voice,

missing you at places we partied

ACKNOWLEDGEMENTS

and joke around.

i don't know how long this will go on for,

all i want is for you to be here with us. "

sometimes there is no definition for time, in happy moments it slips away and when you want it to die it runs away anyway.

Prologue

Love, they say, is blind.

For in its intoxicating embrace, we often fail to see the pitfalls, the shadows that lurk beneath the surface of passionate desire. We stumble headlong into the unknown, our hearts open and vulnerable, only to find ourselves adrift in a sea of unrequited longing.

For love reason often takes a backseat. We surrender to the allure of passion, our senses heightened, our inhibitions fading. We see only the shimmering reflection of our desires, oblivious to the potential for heartbreak that lies beneath the surface. This collection of poems explores the intricate tapestry of love in all its messy, beautiful, and heartbreaking glory.

It delves into the exhilarating highs – the first blush of romance, the intoxicating thrill of shared moments, the whispered secrets that bind two souls together. But it also confronts the agonizing lows – the crushing weight of rejection, the enduring ache of a love lost, the bitter sting of unrequited longing.

Prepare to be swept away by the intoxicating rush of first love, to confront the vulnerabilities that lie beneath the surface, to grapple with the enduring pain of a love that may never be, and ultimately, to discover the enduring power of the human heart, its capacity for both immense joy and profound sorrow.

Lovers Are Blind

1. EYES

When I close my eyes,
I remember your face
Glaring at me.
Our eyes are locked at each other
As if they're in love;
I wish they were.
I look at you,
Driving me away from my worries
So concentrated towards you,
You're still watching me;
But I can't stare too long
Afraid of falling for you again
I feel dumb,
Can't even make eye contact
For more than a couple of seconds;
But I still can't resist myself
And I keep gazing at you,
You keep moistening your lips
And I stare at you
Like a melting scoop of ice-cream
On a pile of hot fudge brownie,
Embarrassing myself.
But I know you know it too

And you let me stalk anyway
As you know I'll miss you
And only remember these glimpses
When we're apart.
~ds

2. WATCHING YOU SLEEP

It's just so peaceful
Admiring you carefree.
Your face half on the pillow,
Your cheeks as if marshmallows.
And your eyes, so dark
Sometimes peeking towards me
Loosing me into you,
My tongue slipping dumb words
Making me forget my verse;
But then, I look at you
And my heart fills up,
Banging my ribs like a drummer
And this mind;
can't stop thinking of touching you,
accidentally touching your feet
or playing with your hair;
it all just feels so ideal to me.
My world would be yours
If you crash into me
As it's already inclined towards you
Even when you're not with me.
~ds

3. WAS IT A CRIME ?

I feel empty inside
But I can feel the rush
Of blood flushing my veins,
Aching my heart.
And I still feel I can take it,
As if a dead soldier
Still walking for loyalty,
Breathing through bullet holes;
It feels as if someone
has removed my heart
from my chest
And asked to take deep breaths.
Is it meaningful to live this life
Where love feels like a crime?
I wish I never told how I felt
As it just made me feel worse,
Knowing that you know
And you still don't care;
Makes me feel open from outside
And broken from inside.
~ds

4. MUNDANE ROUTINE

Pushing out all the serotonin,

Detoxicating my heart

From meaningless hopes;

Pulling in adrenaline

To see a new day.

Feeling the first rays of sun

Enlightening me with its warmth;

Hoping to see a better day

Afterall tired of the same everyday

Killing me with boring days.

Explore myself with passions

I can cave

To find something new,

Something exciting

To see a new ray

The one, that can

Stimulate the everyday.

Still finding joy

In tiny little glimpses

Of joy and laughter

Spreading everywhere;

Where life feels better

Then yesterday.
Sleeping to end this chaos
Of nonsense thoughts.
Trying to escape the ordinary days.
~ds

5. IS IT LOVE ?

I don't know
Is it love or nothing?
As whenever I look at your eyes,
It's as if a pause has taken
All over the world
And it's just us.
Staring at each other,
I seem to get so lost
Still you seem to ignore me
As if I'm nothing to you,
When you know how I feel
And whenever I say something
It's as if I wasn't there at all,
It feels as if you don't even notice me
When I do everything for you.
I don't know
Is it love or nothing?
As I can't seem to loose you
From my mind,
It's as if I'm crazily attached to a magnet
My heart has been pulling me from.
I don't know
If it's love or paradox?

Should I keep desiring your toxicity
And let myself burn with it
Or should I just slam that door
In my head and run away from you
As you'll never see me as I want you to.
~ds

6. SEXY NIGHTMARES

Maybe I'm going crazy,

I keep dreaming about you late nights

And the whole day I try to forget those lies

Trying to avoid thinking about your eyes.

But still at nights you haunt my dreams

Reminding me of those nights.

Things I wish you would've done.

When I knew it wasn't meant to be,

As you don't feel the same about me

It's just me and my unresolved feelings;

But how do I resolve feelings

That I can't feel anymore,

Or maybe I've pushed them away;

Deep in a box

Labelled "Hazardous"

As they were the thorns

Clutching my heart

Into relentless pain.

How will I find peace

Knowing that I'll see you again

Acting as if we were nothing

Just two friends.

~ds

7. DESIRE

Trapped in this chaos of your thoughts;
surrounding me is this loneliness
which craves for your presence.
Is this how my love dies for you?
this connection, just vanished in seconds.
I just want to escape this body faraway
assuming that you'll love me in some others'
But what about love?
is love attached to the body or soul?
Sometimes i feel you're watching me.
I don't know if it's just the desire driving me
or the thought of having you by my side.
It feels hopeless loving you;
but at the same time the happiest,
envisioning being with you.
I don't know how many times
i've been trapped in your cycle,
making me feel crazily obsessed.
I can never stop, no matter how hard
you hurt me.
How can i move on
without thinking about you?
And hating you is just

falling into endless failing cycles.
You're the only one i want
and the only one i can never have.
It devours my heart
that you don't feel the same way
and it's ok, because this love feels endless.
I keep falling for you again and again.
i can feel someone squeezing my heart.
It aches a lot when you ignore me
as if I'm nothing, but how do i tell you
that you're the world to me.
I feel I'll keep failing for you,
I don't know what you wanted from me
or maybe you didn't want anything at all,
No matter what;
in the hope of finding someone like you,
i'll keep bouncing back
as no one will be you.
Was it me, my face
or my body
i don't know
what desired you about me but
I'm still trying to escape you,
making myself do everything
in the hope that you'll see me one day,
As i see you.
~ds

8. JUST FORGET ABOUT IT

Make me forget all those days…
Days, i could see you every day,
Make me forget all those laughs,
all those memories when i was with you.
Make me forget all those drives
And bike rides we went on;
all those unplanned adventures,
in which i craved to be with you.
Make me forget all those times you slept beside me,
while i watched you sleep for hours,
waiting for something to happen between us.
Make me forget how i felt,
when you held my hand
no matter it was for something nonsense
but i can't contemplate how that felt.
Make me forget all those pictures i took of you,
thinking of watching you when you're not there,
it's just meaningless
as my mind is always thinking about you.
Make me forget that i fell in love with you,
and it was so dreadful;
as the hope that you'll love me back never died.

I don't know whether this hope will persist or not,
But my hope for you is already dead.
Just make me forget you!
It seems meaningless loving someone for so long
and waiting for them to like you forever,
as a hopeless romantic.
Just make me forget your face,
as you're the only person i wanted
and i don't want to remember your face
as it will just keep reminding me
that you're not in my life anymore.
After everything that happened between us,
you said "just forget about it- it was a mistake"
that was the moment my love for you started fading;
i just wish i had received the comfort of being loved by you.
At last, you made me forget how to love someone.
~ds

9. THIS WORLD

Stuck at a point,

A sudden flow of guilt

The pressure of future,

And a messed up head.

Trying to resist myself

From those relaxants,

Making me forget all worries

But how can i?

This is my life,

Will have to deal with it someday;

Still loaded from today,

Tears trapped at bay

Paused from dropping

Afraid of this societal judgement day.

The fears never die

Challenging me to overcome those;

I try and fail

But never give up

Knowing that I'm grown up

Will have to fight my way

Through this world anyway

and all I crave is the one,

the only one

I wish to dedicate.
I want to do whatever makes me happy,
Whatever I feel like;
But the problem is
I feel as if I'm living a lie,
Trapped in this hell hole
All by myself
Feeling helpless
Hoping for someone to rescue me
But should I have hope for a saviour?
As this is my life to deal with.
Isn't it meaningless
To think that this life
Is a crafted destiny
If yes, Than whose is this life
The destiny's or mine.
My head can't think straight,
So many thoughts clashing together,
Provoking me to shout my brain out
With the exhaustion
Of everyday's nonsense
But why should i?
Born with a golden feather.
To this world it's just gold and glamour,
But in my heart there's loneliness
It just feels empty
And hollow from any side,

I can't have anyone for myself,
Is this the price for the gold and glamour?
It's as if I have everything but nothing
At the same time.
~ds

10. YOU LEFT

I didn't want to leave you
But you had to.
It's been so many times
That you've broken me,
It doesn't even matter anymore.
I feel the pain
Clutching my heart
But my tears are dried up
They won't fall anymore.
Is it that I'm not in love anymore?
Or that I knew I needed you
but I can't have you?
I tried really hard to disregard you
And not be distracted
But I failed and fell back,
and after all you were gonna go
And that didn't make me sad;
I just wanted to live in the moments
When I felt I had you,
As if they were the last ones;
But they were,
As you left
Not as surprisingly

as you came.

How many times a break up happens?

Until the hearts are broken?

Until the people are.

~ds

11. CHILLING THAT BRAIN

Roaming through a field
I heard water flowing
Through a tiny stream
Floating minerals
With fresh life within.
Birds singing melodies to each other,
Sun calming the winter chills,
Forming fresh dews on tiny leaves;
Swishing wind blew through my ears,
Watching the opaque sky
On a foggy morning
Gazing at tiny sparrows
Chasing each other
In search of love,
Cows mooing
Feeling the warmth of sun
Munching off fresh feed,
Honey bees buzzing
Through the trees
And honey hives,
And there was no need for anything
As the homeostasis couldn't be better enough

And all my mind teased me about

Was that you left me,

Even when you liked me.

How will I ever find reason in that?

~ds

12. A HUG

I missed our last hug,
The only one I could've got from you
And that too I wasted
On a half shoulder hug,
Just because I was worried
Our friends would notice,
But no one cared
They all hugged you correctly
As if they lived miles away
But I missed it
And still regret it
As it would've been the best excuse
To hug you closely.
Never thought
we'd drift so apart.
Sometimes I laugh at myself
Thinking how delusional I got
Dreaming you'd stick up with me
And never let go;
But I guess
fantasies are all they could be
as you moved on
the second I got out of your hair

no pun intended,
as if you were so civil.
Maybe this clinginess
Is what you hated
as you even questioned me
Whether I was still attached?
Well who wouldn't be!
The person you've been waiting for
Your entire life
Suddenly is into you
Though not much, but still.
Of course I had to lie
To keep you tied up
In your own loop.
I guess,
I'll never understand you
And can't seem to forget you too
You keep haunting my dreams
As I would've wanted to
But want to stop those illusions
because there's no room
For meaningless hopes
when you can't even dream me.
~ds

13. MY CUTIE PIE

I tried,
Tried very hard to forget you
But you still fantasize my dreams;
We both were laughing
And you looked so cute,
You knew how much I loved you
But you didn't care
You were still happy.
I just miss your laugh,
The smile that stole my heart,
Those eyes, so dark
That I used to blindly follow
Through unknown paths
To get lost in them
And those lips, for which
I can't find words to class.
If I could just hold your hands
And feel that soft skin of yours.
I just miss **you** a lot,
I wish I could hug you once;
Once and for all
As tight as it can be
And feel your arms around me

As last time I missed it,

That could've been my last chance

To hug you as **friends**

As we parted ways

To be faraway.

~ds

14. AURORA LIGHTS

You stole me again,
After I had already lost you
From my mind.
Why? Why did you have to?
I got trapped in your love
Just as you passed a bit of light;
I dived into your ocean
Trying to find that light;
The light which shows you
How much I loved you
In my life.
In the hope of making you fall
I sank deep, so deep that I can't find myself,
nor you too, or that light.
I can't seem to feel you,
It's as if my first love
Robbed me from me;
And now you roam freely,
Having drinks with your fake ones
Who always seem to fall for your trust
But you just play with them
Just as you did me first.
I tried to manipulate you

Into my games

But you cheated

And won the race.

I'm done playing those games,

Trying to find that light

As I had hope of **us**

but there wasn't any light,

just an illusion.

Since **I** was so crazy in love

I forgot that there was only me,

Loving a dove.

~ds

15. LIVING A LIE

Done waiting for those aurora lights
That one day you will see me
Through those ocean deep eyes
As that's what I craved since eternity
Crying sleepless nights.
I tried, tried to be your friend this time
But after all, you found someone else
Making me your use and throw trash;
While I thought you liked me
You casually hopped to someone else;
Really tore my last shreds of hope this time
Reminding me of the reality
And the truth,
That it was only me
Living this lie
While you couldn't even think of us tie.
~ds

16. MAYBE IN A PARALLEL UNIVERSE

Maybe in a parallel universe
you'd be mine
And I'd be yours,
You'd kiss me and love me
As I want now,
Not only in my dreams.
I wish that universe could be this one.
Hugging you for so long
Without realising how long it has been,
It won't matter
As we would have all the time in the world
And much less to care about others;
I wish that could be us.
Maybe in a parallel universe
You'd love me the same way I do,
Maybe you'd see me
The way I look at you.
Maybe I'd be the perfection
To your imperfections.
Maybe in a parallel universe
You won't be able to resist me;
The way I can't resist your presence

No matter how hard you hurt me
As my heart belongs to you.
Maybe in a parallel universe
You'll think about me
And miss me the same way I do.
Maybe you'll cry a few drops for me
Compared to my unnecessary rivers.
Maybe you'd want to kiss me
As much as I want to.
Maybe you'll understand
Why I ignored staring at your eyes for long
As I knew I'd fall for you again.
Maybe in a parallel universe
We are together,
You're mine and I'm yours;
You'll be the reality
To my delusions
And the same softy I fell for;
Maybe in a parallel universe.
~ds

17. WHY CAN'T I ?

Why can't I stop imagining us?
Even when I distract myself
From my thoughts,
I still see you in my dreams;
Harassing me for my dreams to come true
Or enabling them as a possibility,
Especially on the days
When I try to forget you,
As if it's a sign that I shouldn't.
I still try to forget you in my dreams
As I mind it!
I'm tired of this toxicity
Which I called love;
But anyway,
my mind controls me
Though my consciousness
doesn't want you
A small part of my unconscious brain
Still craves you
For nothingness
which you deliver.
~ds

18. THE VIRTUAL REALITY

I feel stuck at a point;
Clashing memories in my head
Not letting me think straight,
As if trapped in an hourglass
Where all I can see is my reflection
Which is also virtual.
Sometimes I feel,
I've been dreaming so much
I feel as if everything is slowly fading,
I don't even recognise the truth anymore,
It's as if I've been dreaming my fantasies;
which I don't have the guts for.
Even though most of the times I forget my dreams
Still they feel real.
Still some of the parts
Are stuck in my memory
As if they happened.
Or was it just an unconscious memory
Stuck in my virtual reality.
~ds

19. LOSS OF LOVE

You keep breaking my heart
Again and again
And I keep mending it
Back to back,
Just in hope to love you some more;
One day this cycle will end
When I won't be able to mend it anymore
And won't fall for anyone
As all I'll be is heartless,
Just as you are.
You don't know how it feels
To love someone so bad
And crush your own heart,
Just because
You were ready to give it away
No matter that person
Doesn't care for your heart
But nor you,
As you're just a lost cause for them.
When they want nothing to do with you
But you still keep falling
Into endless traps
And keep smashing your head to a mirror

Trying to change yourself for them
When you know you can't.
I wish you fall so crazy in love,
Just like me.
As if, you feel
They're the one you're here for
And then you'll understand
What I felt.
Having someone by your side
And thinking they're your whole world.
I'll never forget those days
When you slept by my side
And didn't mind
When our toes touched.
I hope you feel the loss of love
As that's the pain
That can never be felt by words.
Well, I loved you
And you never loved me back
But I wish you get someone
Who you love so bad
And you'll be stuck in the same pond
When they jump off
And you'll have to bear
For the one you fell for.
~ds

20. MINDLESS DREAMS

Had a dream.
I, as always
Trying to hate you;
Consciously to move on,
Was still mad at you,
Even in my dreams.
Unconsciously unaware
falling into your fish trap again.
You were doing something illicit openly
And I trapped, was an accomplice
Still warning your actions.
Foreseen we get caught;
They were taking me away
While You, fighting for me
As you cared
And out of the blue you get shot!
And it all came back to me,
Realised how much I loved you
And felt that it hadn't gone away at all.
The whole thing was just an act
After all those myriad struggles
And sleepless nights of your thoughts.

I don't know why my mind
Tortures me as if I'm blind,
I felt dead after you passed.
The anger and grief swallowed me;
Became a deadly maniac,
You know I'm not that vicious.
Cried, cried the whole damn dam
And the anger poured into the flood,
Killed your killer!
Still didn't get you!
As if I ever did.
Did that dream signify
That the **us** I've been living is over
Or that I shouldn't forget you?
How do I take meaning
From such overzealous dream.
I've been trying not to dream you
Or even think about you
And now this!
How do I blast off this?
Maybe my mind is screening
A part of me will always love you
No matter you won't;
Just realised how will I live my life
As I always imagined
For you to be in my life
But dreams don't come true.

~ds

21. OVERTHINKING PIT

It's scary and terrifying for me
To leave you
And at the same time
So ordinary and casual for you
To leave me.
I don't know what to think,
I can't seem to think about anything
Except you.
So not ghosting my brain
Unlike your everyday ghosting.
I just want to feel you beside me
And hug you one last time
Before you leave,
As I don't know
If I'll ever see you again
And I'm horrified by that;
It's as if you're my lifeline
And I'm just a stranger to you.
After all I perceived
That I've barely moved an inch from you
And you'll always be a soft pillow
Comforting my heart,

Even though you won't be mine
And I'll never be yours
But you'll always be in my heart
Or somewhere in my soul,
If love is really bonded
Not just to the bodies,
As I believe.
I don't know what I feel,
How can I express myself
Without knowing how I feel,
When it just feels lonely
And tired of feeling
Stupid pity for myself,
It feels hopeless
When you have so many hands around
But none to hold yours.
Every love story
doesn't have to be
A happy ending
It just ends when peace is procured.
Sometimes love is the problem
And sometimes it's the only solution
But in this story
There was only me
Never **us.**
Is love a lie?
Because it feels like

I was definitely living one.
Love is never a lie,
Even when you don't receive it back;
It's enough that you feel it
As you're the creator of that art.
~ds

22. DEAD CHAPTER

I feel like you don't like me anymore.

You don't even look at me,

You run away from me.

Wherever you go

I rush back to you

Like your lap dog

but still you leave;

done playing this tom & jerry

you're not worth the pain.

There's just one thing

I'm grateful you gave me,

You taught me how to love myself

And then I realised

How easy it was to love me

Rather than your ungratefulness

And it was easier to leave you

As you did me.

It's all over now

I finally got the guts

And told you

That I don't give any damn ducks

For you anymore.

Though I did a bit

In that moment
But now I don't care
And I won't
As you didn't ever.
Just called me once
Didn't even try again
And then I reaped
How badly I tried this venom
The one that I craved so much
That turned into
A dead addiction.
Was tired of your toxicity.
The one who wanted to dive into every pond
Bubbling with other fishes,
Needed some fresh air now
Felt like even you knew the intensity
With which I jumped off your jolly train
Where everyone seems happy
But are dead inside.
For the first time
Started to feel something
Without you in my life
Though a few days were traumatic
And had loud outbursts.
Embracing thy peace now
Though don't want to think about you,
Immerse myself into work

Still dreaming you in nightmares
But stopped enjoying those
As I perceived,
Though it was all real
It was always delusional for you.
I remember and crack at myself
How badly I begged for you,
Praising the lord
As the one thing I want
In this world.
So selfish of me
To waste my time
On a poison for myself
~ds

23. DISTRACTION THERAPY

As I took the road never travelled before

Discovering antiques for my collection;

I walked through moist soil

And grass as soft as dove's feathers,

Through foamy beaches to collect

Sea shells and dead corals,

I felt a salty breeze

As I watched the last rays of sun

Glaring at me.

I walked through a wild forest

Trying to get lost in itself;

In the hope of forgetting you

Watching those bees

sucking nectar out of lilies,

by the lily pond I sat

staring at the fishes make bubbles;

I saw my reflection in the water

And I still wasn't satisfied with the serenity

As all my mind wandered about

Was what you felt for me.

~ds

24. THINGS WE DO FOR LOVE

Is love enough? Is it?
It wonders me a lot
Which is most crucial
Love or hope?
Hope is the one
By which we live
And love is the one
For which we live;
But what happens
When there's no hope for love?
There were times
When I lost hopes for you,
But those birds came back to me
As my blind heart
Forgave you even after
You broke it into shreds.
Hopefully my mind
Controls me
From diving into meaningless hopes
And one bloody heart
Which is soft and sharp,
But not mine to keep.

I've made peace with you
Even when I tried to hurt you
And said stuff out of jealousy;
Trying to break stuff with you forever
And later apologised for my mess
And I know you'll never forgive me
For what I said,
But I don't care now
Nor do you after all that happened;
This was the only way
We couldn't have talked
No matter peace took the space
In my heart at your place
And I feel you hate me
But I'll always regret the words I said
And I'm sorry
That I never saw you,
Just as a friend.
Somewhere in a corner of my heart
I do feel losing a friend forever,
But I had to lose you
To take my heart back from you,
Not the one I craved to be mine
As you didn't throw yours;
Nor did you catch mine,
Just the one
Which was mine.

~ds

THE END

About The Author

Dhyan Sompura: A Poet Exploring Depths of Love.

Dhyan Sompura, a young writer and artist currently preparing for his Master's degree, continues to explore the depths of human emotion through his poetry. Having recently completed his

Bachelor's degree in Pune, he now resides in Thangadh with his family.

Dhyan's literary journey began with a focus on unfettered expression, venturing beyond the confines of traditional rhyming schemes. As his skills matured, he embraced the power of rhyme while never losing sight of the raw, unfiltered essence of his words. His poems transcend mere description, delving into the complexities of human emotions with a depth and seriousness that resonates with readers who have experienced life's profound moments.

"Lovers Are Blind" is a testament to Dhyan's ability to capture the bittersweet reality of love, particularly the poignant ache of unrequited affection. He eschews superficial rhymes, opting instead for a focus on the true meaning of words. The poems delve into the intricate details of heartbreak, contrasting them with fleeting glimpses of joy. This portrayal reflects Dhyan's keen understanding of the one-sided love experience, where the intensity of emotions is amplified by the lack of reciprocation.

Dhyan's creative spirit extends beyond poetry. At the age of 13, he penned a fictional story, "Frozen Wild," highlighting his deep connection to nature. This connection is further evident in his breathtaking artwork, showcased on various social media platforms (@art_defines_nature) and his personal website. He is also a prolific blogger, sharing his thoughts and experiences on his platform,

"Emotions Through Words"
(https://emotionthroughwords.wordpress.com/).

"Lovers Are Blind" marks Dhyan's second published solo collection, following the collaborative success of "Those Tiny Little Moments" with Radhika Limbasiya. This new offering promises a journey into the heart's most vulnerable chambers, resonating with those who have loved and lost, or perhaps, loved without return.

Contact info-

E-mail: sompuradhyan@gmail.com

Instagram acc: @dhatz_meee

writing acc: @emotions__through.words

Notes